Contents

Introduction

There has been much discussion about the differences between boys and girls, and scientists now conclude that although there is little difference in the physical structure of the brains, there is often a great difference in the way boys and girls learn and approach new activities. Parents and practitioners everywhere are well aware of these differences: boys are generally more interested in active play, in the outdoors and in being with groups of other boys, often out of range of adults; many girls prefer to be near adults, choosing more sedentary activities, and watching adults closely, modelling them in their own play. Most girls also develop the ability to sit still and control their hands and fingers earlier than boys, and this often means that girls choose more quiet activities that make best use of these skills. Another factor is that most early years practitioners are female, with feminine likes and dislikes and a female view of the world, which sometimes results in a lack of understanding of the needs of the boys they work with.

Our suggestions in this book are that adventurous and active projects where adults and children work and play together, particularly out of doors, may better meet the needs of adventurous and active children, as well as increasing the value placed on these activities by some adults. Practitioners tell us that they sometimes find it difficult to think of genuinely adventurous activities which meet the needs of the boys in their groups, while accepting the restrictions of staffing and resources in their settings.

Of course, we would never suggest that you deter girls from joining or initiating these activities, and some girls are themselves very adventurous! So despite the title, please use the activities flexibly, and make sure the children never think that there are some activities just for girls and some just for boys.

We have introduced some more challenging activities and some less familiar resources and equipment, but most of the things you need will be available already in your setting or can be collected from bargain sources, recycled materials and by asking parents and families for unwanted objects.

Handling tools and materials

Natural materials - Some activities involve working with mud, sand, stones twigs and sticks. Train children to wash their hands after using natural materials, and make sure they know never to use these things to hurt or endanger others.

Tools - Some of the activities in this book may need you to expand the range of tools available to the children in your setting. We would advise you to buy the best quality you can afford, as these will last longer and be safer than cheaper versions. There are many suppliers of these tools, and we have given you some websites to consider. Using real tools (small hammers, screwdrivers, saws, pliers and safe knives) is fascinating for young children, and can be built into your daily programme. Make time at the beginning of the year to explain the risks to children and train them in the use of tools.

Outdoor space - We have suggested that most of the activities can be done out of doors, and the attraction of making, doing and experimenting outside will make activities even more attractive to those children who prefer to spend their time in the open air. Many of the activities take an indoor idea and expand it so that it can be done on a bigger scale or with larger equipment outside.

Some settings have restricted space available for outdoor play, but if you can provide a permanent place in your outdoor area for making, doing and experimenting, you will find that boisterous activity can easily be channelled

New resources and ingredients - Most children are familiar with dough, flour, sand, different kinds of tape, paint and glue. The activities in this book expand the range by suggesting simple ideas for introducing plaster, plaster bandage, ice, metal, wire, papier mâché, etc. Where these need high levels of adult support or additional guidance, we have indicated this in the text. However, children soon become confident in these new methods, and will quickly incorporate them into their free play.

Early science - Many of the activities, although they may appear to be focused on creative development, offer early scientific experiences, which will be consolidated as children move through the education system. It is important to use proper scientific language and to encourage children to look closely at how things change when mixed, diluted, dissolved or dried. Give the children time to watch and talk about what is happening, discuss the activities and get involved in 'sustained shared thinking', which is at the heart of real learning.

into more creative pursuits. Make these materials and equipment available on trolleys, in baskets and boxes or lightweight tables, so that the children can select these in their independent play. The equipment can be brought indoors by the children at the end of the session. Keep the interest going by adding new resources, teaching new techniques and ideas, or offering new tools. Many of the activities can be offered for independent play, after a short introduction from you; some need a little more adult support, and some need you to be available all the time.

Useful websites

These websites suggest resources and links to further ideas:

Food colouring and a wide range of simple science resources:
www.tts-group.co.uk

A good range of interesting resources for out of doors:
www.mindstretchers.co.uk

Plaster bandage and craft plaster:
www.amazon.co.uk

Craft materials in bulk:
http://www.bakerross.co.uk or
http://www.hobbycraft.co.uk

Forest School equipment and resources, bags, collecting pots, magnifying glasses, rubber mallets and clothing:
http://www.muddyfaces.co.uk

Mud kitchen tools and kits:
http://www.muddyfaces.co.uk

Small woodworking tools:
http://www.mulberrybush.co.uk
www.fredaldous.co.uk
www.spottygreenfrog.co.uk
or
www.bristoltools.co.uk

Living willow:
http://thewillowbank.com

A wide range of tough cameras and DVD cameras for children:
http://www.digitalblue.org.uk

Useful publications

Books

These books have more ideas for investigative and creative learning:

- The Little Book of Dough
- The Little Book of Free and Found
- The Little Book of Investigations
- The Little Book of Explorations

All from www.bloomsbury.com/featherstone

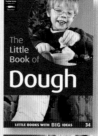

Background reading

Good practice in early years woodwork:
http://www.nurseryworld.co.uk/article/1131490/eyfs-best-practice-woodwork

Mud kitchens:
www.muddyfaces.co.uk/mud_kitchens.php

Food allergy alert

When using food stuffs to enhance your play opportunties, always be mindful of potential food allergies. We have used this symbol on the relevant pages.

FOOD allergy !

Skin allergy alert

Some detergents and soaps can cause skin reactions. Always be mindful of potential skin allergies when letting children mix anything with their hands, and always provide facilities to wash materials off after they have been in contact with skin. Watch out for this symbol on the relevant pages.

SKIN allergy !

Safety issues

Social development can only take place when children can experiment and take reasonable risks in a safe environment. Encouraging independence and the use of natural resources inevitably raises some health and safety issues; these are identified where appropriate.

Children need help and good models for washing their hands when using natural materials or preparing food. They may need reminding not to put things in their mouths, and to be careful with real-life or found resources.

SAFETY FiRST!

50 fantastic ideas to captivate boys

Making magic

Make your own magic wand

What you need:

- **Some straight sticks about 20-25 cm long**
- **Children's gardening gloves, and an adult pair for you**
- **Safe knives** (blunt table knives are ideal)
- **Secateurs** (for adult use, stubborn side twigs)
- **Permanent markers or paint** (optional)

Top tip ⭐

Why not use this activity in a 'Dads and lads' session for boys and their dads?

Taking it forward

- Make some wizard cloaks from black material and kit out your outdoor role-play area to look like a magic den, with potion bottles, bowls, spell books and other objects.
- Write spells for the children to say as they use the wands. Join in yourself!

What's in it for the children?

Making wands will help with fine motor control, and using them will give opportunities to experiment with words and movements.

✚ Health & Safety

Any activity involving knives must be carefully supervised. Children must sit down when using them, and should never be left without an adult.

What to do:

1. Explain to the children that you are going out to collect sticks to make wands. Make sure they know how to carry a stick, and emphasise that they are not weapons!

2. Go for a walk in the woods, the park or the grounds of your setting, and collect some suitable sticks. They should be straight and preferably tapering towards the end. Rotten wood is unsuitable. Make sure you get some extra sticks in case of breakage!

3. Take your sticks back to your setting and talk to the children about the following safety rules when using knives:

   a. always sit down when using a knife

   b. use gloves

   c. always cut away from your body

   d. make sure you have plenty of room

   e. never use your knife to play games or threaten anyone.

4. Put gloves on, and show the children how to strip the bark from their stick by carefully using the knife to ease it from the wood, always working away from their body.

5. When the white core wood is exposed and all the bark is removed, polish the 'wand' with your glove.

6. Decorate the wand with felt pens, or dip your wand in paint.

7. Talk about playing safely with the wands. Make sure children know that wands do not touch others; the magic goes through the air! Make a special magical place to use the wands, and limit the number of children who can play there at any time.

Disappearing tricks
Investigating how things dissolve

What you need:

- Saucers, small bowls or jars
- Clear plastic containers with screw tops, such as water bottles
- Plastic jugs for water
- Funnels
- Teaspoons
- Magnifying glasses
- Things to mix: salt, brown and white sugar, instant coffee, sand, lemonade crystals, mud, flour, powdered milk, toothpaste, soap
- A camera

What to do:

1. Set all the things out on a table, outside or indoors.

2. Look at the resources together and explain that this is an experiment table for scientists. Tell the children you would like to find out what happens when you mix things with water.

3. Look at, and name, all the substances on the table; then show the children how they can pour water into the bottles, add substances and put on the top. What do they think will happen if they shake the bottle? What do they think happens if they stop shaking and watch the liquid?

4. Sit with the children as they begin to experiment. Take photos and offer the camera to the children to use too.

5. Let children find other substances to experiment with.

6. Children should wash their own bottles and tidy up when they have finished. You will need to top up the equipment and substances ready for the next group – children will use all you can offer!

Top tip ★
Make sure you include some things that don't dissolve, e.g. sand.

Taking it forward

- Try the experiments using glue, dough, cellulose paste, sequins, grass or powder paint.
- Get some mud from the garden and mix it with water in a big jar with a screw top. Shake it up and then watch it settle. Talk about why it settles in layers.

What's in it for the children?

Children need plenty of experience of these simple experiments with real substances and objects, looking carefully at what happens and learning new words such as 'dissolve', 'soluble', 'float', 'sink', etc.

✚ Health & Safety
Make sure children understand that they should not eat the things they are using.

Creepy crawly
Making a home for spiders

What you need:

- A plastic aquarium with a top, or a sheet of plastic to cover it
- A large glass or jar and a piece of card, or a 'pooter' (a special tool for catching minibeasts)
- Some stones, twigs and leaves
- Magnifying glasses

Taking it forward

- Tell stories and sing songs about spiders. Draw pictures and make some big spider webs outside, using string or wool tied to the climbing apparatus or the building.
- Catch other minibeasts: ants, woodlice, earwigs, worms, beetles, slugs and snails. Always return them after just a few days.

What's in it for the children?

Watching minibeasts is a fascinating activity and teaches children how to care for living things. It also helps some children to deal with their fears and anxieties.

Top tip ⭐

Many adults dislike spiders. Make sure you don't let your feelings influence the children. If in doubt, ask an adult who is comfortable with spiders to lead this activity.

✚ Health & Safety

Make sure the container is securely located in a position where the children can watch the spider without letting it escape.

What to do:

1. Talk with the children about the 'spidery' you are going to set up together and explain what you are going to do. Talk about being kind to creatures, even if you are scared of them.

2. Prepare the home for the spiders with sticks, stones, mud and leaves.

3. Now let the children help you to find some places in your setting or the outdoor area where spiders might be living. Watch these places (behind bins, under logs and stones, on fences and bushes) until you find some spiders. Look at them in their own habitat and take some photos, so you can make their new home comfortable for them.

4. Use a glass, jar or bug catcher to catch your spider and transfer it to the aquarium. Be careful – their legs are easily damaged.

5. Cover the 'spidery' securely and watch the spiders as they explore their new home.

6. When you have looked at the spiders, release them where you found them. Don't keep them captive for more than a couple of days.

7. As a further activity, catch some other minibeasts to watch.

How does it work?

Investigating by dismantling things

What you need:

- Some of the following:
  - wind-up clocks and watches
  - radios, tape recorders, vacuum cleaners
  - remote controls, computer keyboards
  - bikes, trikes, scooters
  - broken electronic or clockwork toys
- Small screwdrivers, pliers and wire cutters
- Plastic or polystyrene trays for parts
- A camera

What to do:

1. Sit together and look at the things you have brought. Tell the children that they can take these things apart because they are old and no one wants them anymore.

2. Make sure they understand the difference between taking things apart and just destroying them. Talk about how to keep the bits they remove in a tray or box, so they know which bits came from which item.

3. Examine and name all the tools and make sure the children know how to use them safely.

4. Now let them start to work alone or in pairs to dismantle the equipment and objects, using the tools, and asking for help if they need it. They may need help when it gets difficult (tight screws, etc.).

5. Talk about what is happening. Make sure you or they take a photo of their object before and after dismantling it, and take photos as they take it apart. Stay with the children as they work, to listen to and join in with the discussion.

6. Ask children to talk to the whole group about what they have found, using the photos.

Taking it forward

- As a further activity, make some photo sequences of the dismantling, for photo books or Powerpoint presentations.

- Use the internet to find some 'exploded diagrams' of engines or other machines. Offer big sheets of paper and fine black felt pens so children can try doing labelled diagrams themselves.

What's in it for the children?

Children will begin to think beyond what they can see from the outside of an object.

Health & Safety

Choose your item carefully as some are specially made so they don't come apart. Always remove batteries before giving the items to children to explore.

Top tip ★

Look in charity shops, junk shops and on market stalls for objects to dismantle. Market stallholders are often generous if you say the items are for children to use!

Superheroes come alive
Make a superhero collage

What you need:

- Lots of images of superheroes from:
  - superhero comics, magazines, colouring books
  - gift wrap and cards
  - clip art
- Basket/box or builder's tray
- Masking tape and scissors
- White glue mixed with water
- Spreaders or brushes
- A black bin-liner, opened out flat to make a big sheet
- Felt pens

Top tip ⭐

Use cheap colouring books, then the children can colour in the pictures afterwards.

Taking it forward

- Use a pop-up tent to make your role-play area into a superhero cave, with your collage displayed at the back. Make masks, hoods and armbands.

- Use the same method to make 'stained glass' windows, using torn tissue paper. Overlap the tissue to make extra colours and mount it in your windows.

What's in it for the children?

Celebrating popular culture is a good way to engage children in activities using fine motor control.

What to do:

1. Spread the black plastic over a table and tape it down.

2. Show the children the comics and other pictures you have collected. Talk about superheroes and explain that they could make a really big superhero picture together for your room or your role-play area.

3. Explain that after they have cut out pictures from the comics and other papers, they should stick them on the black plastic.

4. Offer all the comics and other pictures in a basket or box, perhaps in a builder's tray.

5. Let the children get on with talking, choosing, cutting and sticking. Visit them regularly, but you do not need to be there all the time.

6. Encourage the children to cover the black plastic all over, so there are no gaps at all. Use plenty of glue under and on top of the pictures to fix them down firmly. This is important for the finished product.

7. When the black plastic is totally covered with pictures, help the children to put a final layer of dilute white glue over the whole thing and leave it to dry.

8. When the glue is dry and transparent you can peel your collage off the plastic, colour the pictures, and hang or pin it up.

Stick it on, stick it in
Making structures with sticks and peas

What you need:

- **Packs of dried peas**
- **Cocktail sticks** (plenty)
- **Water**
- **A container for soaking the peas**
- **Somewhere to keep the constructions**

Top tip ⭐

If your children get really involved in this activity, you will need lots of peas - try a cash-and-carry for big packs of dried peas or chickpeas.

Taking it forward

- Use sticks and peas to make bridges and buildings for play people or other small world figures.

- Look at the difference between the sticks and peas and commercial construction toys, such as Construct-o-Straws, K'nex, Brio, Meccano, etc.

What's in it for the children?

It's important that children have plenty of practice using their fingers and thumbs. This will help with writing skills later on.

Health & Safety

Cocktail sticks are sharp, so when using them children must learn how to take care so they don't hurt themselves or others.

What to do:

1. Look at the dried peas together and feel their texture. Talk about what they look and feel like, and how they got to be so hard and small.

2. Let the children help you to put the peas in water to soak. Leave them overnight.

3. Drain the peas and look at them again. How are they different? What has happened? Where has all the water gone? Feel the peas again. Do they feel different?

4. Show the children how you can fix the peas together, using the cocktail sticks. Remind them about safety with the sticks.

5. Let them explore the peas and sticks as they make constructions.

6. When they have finished a construction, put it somewhere safe to dry. As the peas dry out again the sticks will become firmly trapped.

7. Look at the constructions together and talk about what you have done.

8. Take some photos and look on the internet for images of buildings made like this; search for 'geodesic dome'.

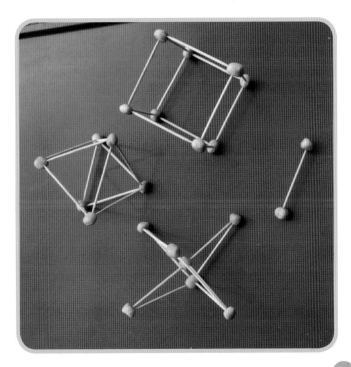

Swinging sand

More work with pendulums

What you need:

- A large empty water bottle
- Scissors or a craft knife
- Strong string
- A broom handle (or long pole) and two chairs
- Powder paint
- Dry sand or salt
- A large sheet of strong paper or card

What to do:

1. Make the frame for the pendulum by tying a pole firmly to the backs of two chairs.

2. Help the children to mix some dry sand or salt with some powder paint in a bowl or bucket.

3. Now let the children help to make your pendulum by cutting the bottom out of the bottle, and making a small hole in the cap. Experiment with the hole, so it is the right size for the sand to flow through. (Practise over the bucket!)

4. Make three holes around the open end of the bottle and hang the empty pendulum upside down from the pole with string (see photo).

5. Put a big sheet of paper or card on the floor, underneath the pendulum.

6. Now put a finger over the hole in the bottle cap and half fill the bottle with coloured sand/salt.

7. Take the finger from the end and give the pendulum a gentle push to swing it over the paper.

8. Watch what happens!

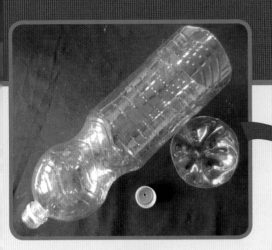

✚ Health & Safety

Make sure the structure is firm and won't fall or get knocked over.

Taking it forward

- Make pendulum patterns with paint and cornflour, or dry salt and powder paint. Swing these over a big sheet painted with dilute white glue. When the pendulum stops, tip off the extra sand and see the pendulum pattern.

- Try suspending paintbrushes from strings and swinging these over the paper.

What's in it for the children?

Watching the objects and the patterns they make helps children experience the effects of motion.

Top tip ⭐

To make a hole in a bottle top or any other hard object, put the top on a lump of playdough and push scissors or a screwdriver through the top into the dough.

Smash it up!
Chalk painting

What you need:

- Coloured chalk
- Heavy zip-lock plastic bags
- Hammers, mallets or big wooden bricks
- Plastic jars or small buckets
- Water
- Paintbrushes
- Cornflour (optional)

What to do:

1. Show the children the pavement chalk and ask them if they know of a way to turn it into paint. Accept and discuss all suggestions, and try a few.

2. Now break some of the chalk and put it in a zip-lock bag. Show the children how to hammer it to a fine powder. Talk about how to use the hammer safely, and remind them to keep their fingers out of the way.

3. Let the children help to make several different bags of smashed chalk and tip them into jars or buckets. Add water, a little at a time, and stir to mix, until your colours have the consistency of paint.

4. Use your chalky paint to make pictures or patterns on the yard, playground or patio.

5. Add some cornflour to the chalky paint and explore the difference in colour and texture: the cornflour should make the paint shiny.

6. Use a hose to wash away the pictures when you have finished, or at the end of a session. Children will enjoy this!

Top tip ⭐

Try 'pound' shops for cheap, coloured pavement chalk.

Taking it forward

- Use this temporary chalk paint to make pictures on your fence or shed.
- Make tracks and roadways on the path or patio for trains or cars to drive along.

What's in it for the children?

Transforming one thing into another helps children to begin to understand the properties of different materials and how they can be changed.

 Health & Safety

Teach children how to use tools safely. Supervise the use of hammers.

Let's hammer
Play safely with hammers and nails

What you need:

- A large sheet of softwood or chipboard at least 2cm thick
- Short nails with big heads (2–2 ½ cm 'clout' nails)
- Hammers and fine-nosed pliers – several of each
- Safety glasses
- Thick elastic bands, string or wool

What to do:

1. Help the children to put the big board in a safe and steady place, on the ground outdoors.

2. Draw a chalk line or put a rope on the ground around the area so other children can watch from a safe distance.

3. Show the children the hammers and nails and demonstrate their safe use. When children first use these, teach them to hold the nail steady using the pliers. You may have to hold the pliers for them until they learn how to do it themselves.

4. Let the children hammer the nails in anywhere they like on the board. Don't hammer the nails all the way into the wood (if the pliers are kept in place it will stop this happening).

5. Stay close to ensure safe working.

6. When the board has plenty of nails, leave it on the ground or stand it on one edge in a safe place, so the children can make patterns from nail to nail with string, wool or elastic bands.

Top tip ⭐

Do this on the ground or the grass, so if nails do go right through, you won't damage your tables.

Taking it forward

- Make another board, and this time paint it or cover it with a collage before you start hammering.
- Get a big log or tree stump and use this for hammering practice.

What's in it for the children?

The hand-eye co-ordination needed for hammering will be good practice for any other activity needing fine motor control, such as writing.

Health & Safety

Always show children the safe way to use tools, and insist that they follow safety rules.

Transform a tin

Create a tin lantern

What you need:

- The use of a freezer
- Small, clean metal cans, with the labels removed
- Oven gloves
- Towels or face flannels
- Big nails, long enough to hold while hammering
- Paint mixed with white glue (optional)

Taking it forward

- Hang the lanterns in the windows of your setting so the sun can shine through them.

- Buy a cheap set of Christmas lights (large bulbs) and tie a lantern over each light so the coloured light shows through.

What's in it for the children?

Making gifts is a great activity and this is one that will appeal especially to boys, who often find card-making less interesting.

Health & Safety

The open end of the tin and the insides where the holes have been punched can be sharp and scratchy. Warn the children, and smooth any rough edges by running a heavy spoon handle over them.

What to do:

1. Wash and check each tin before use (see Health & Safety).

2. Explain that you are going to make a tin lantern but they will have to wait for the cans to freeze before they can make them. It will take at least 24 hours.

3. If you have a freezer at your setting, help the children to fill a can each with water and place it in the freezer. (If you have to freeze the cans at home, bring them in a few at a time in a cool box with freezer blocks.)

4. Explain to the children that they must work in small groups so that an adult can help them all.

5. Put each can on its side on a folded towel or flannel.

6. Let the children use a hammer and a big nail to hammer holes in the can, anywhere they want.

7. Turn the can for them, or let them do it, using an oven glove.

8. When it's finished, they can hammer a hole into the middle of the bottom of the can so it can be hung from a string.

9. Put the can in the water tray or sink until all the ice melts. Then hold the can up to see the hammer patterns.

10. Leave the cans to dry, then decorate with paint if you wish.

11. Children can take the lanterns home, and can also position them upright and use them with tealights or candles.

Top tip ⭐

Remove label glue with sticky remover spray or white spirit (adult only).

Wonderful wire
Simple wire sculpture

What you need:

- **Electrical cable with several wires inside a covering** (computer ethernet cable is suitable)
- **Small wire cutters**
- **Scissors**
- **Plaster of Paris**
- **Mixing bowls**
- **A measuring cup** (e.g. an empty yogurt pot)
- **Individual juice or milk cartons**
- **Paint, beads, ribbon**

Top tip ⭐

If you have spare plaster, do not pour it down the drain as it will block your sink! Let it dry in the bowl, then pop it out. Pour away waste water from the plaster outside (in small quantities it won't do any harm).

Taking it forward

- If you don't want to use plaster of Paris, you can fill the cartons with salt and flour play dough or plasticene. Much younger children could simply work with a lump of dough and ready-cut wires.

What's in it for the children?

Manipulating the wire is an enjoyable way of strengthening muscles in fingers and hands.

✚ Health & Safety

Take care with wire, and don't strip the coating off the inner coloured wires as they are very fine and sharp.

What to do:

1. Cut the tops off the juice cartons.

2. Help the children to cut some pieces of wire of different lengths (about 10–15 cm) and colours, using scissors or wire cutters.

3. Bend some of the wires into shapes or coil some round a pencil to make spirals.

4. Now the adult can mix one cup of plaster with half a cup of water in a bowl (this should be enough for four cartons). Let the children watch this, but it is definitely an adult job.

5. Pour the plaster into the cartons and let the children feel the outside of their carton with their hands – it will get warm!

6. As the plaster hardens, the children can stick the wires into the plaster. They will feel the plaster getting harder each time, so they will need to work quickly.

7. When the plaster is too hard for more wires to be added the children can bend the wires into shapes and decorate each one with beads or ribbons.

8. When the plaster is completely dry and hard, tear away the cartons. Paint the plaster and, if you like, decorate it.

The mud lab

A variation on a mud kitchen

What you need:

- An old table, a big plank between two tables, or an old kitchen cabinet with cupboards underneath
- A bowl, bucket of water, or an old sink unit with a draining board
- A couple of bags of soil-based (not peat) potting compost
- Mud-play tools: scoops, fish slices, spatulas, sieves, colanders, potato mashers, slotted spoons and old saucepans
- Experimenting tools: magnifying glasses, bottles, tubing, plastic syringes and pipettes, plastic test tubes
- Clear plastic containers, jugs, bowls and plastic bottles
- Lab jackets: white shirts with the bottoms and sleeves cut off
- Safety goggles
- Clipboards and ballpoint pens

What to do:

1. Talk about scientists and what they do. You may want to show a DVD or a book about scientists. Say you are going to set up a mud scientists' lab to find out all about mud.

2. Let the children decide where the 'mud lab' will be and what they will need.

3. Make sure the children know the rules for being in the mud lab: keeping the mud in the lab, clearing up the lab and washing your hands when you have finished.

4. When your lab is ready, set the first challenge. Here are some ideas, you will have many more:
   - What is mud made from?
   - Can you make coloured mud?
   - Mix some mud with water. How can you get the water out again?
   - Which tool is best for mixing mud and water?
   - Can you write your name with mud? How did you do it?

5. Refresh your 'mud lab' regularly with new challenges, materials and experiences.

Top tip ⭐
Old furniture from the home corner is ideal for this activity.

Taking it forward

- Mix things with mud: dry soil and cooking oil will make muddy paint; cornflour and washing-up liquid will make shiny paint; white glue will make the mud sticky so the children can mould it into mud pies.
- Use big brushes to paint with watery mud on walls and fences.

What's in it for the children?

Early experiments look just like this, for adult scientists as well as children.

➕ Health & Safety
Always use compost from a garden centre, as it will have been sterilised.

Pirate treasure

Make a chest for your special treasures

What you need:

- Kitchen foil
- Cereal boxes, newspaper
- White glue, scissors, brushes
- Sticky tape
- Hook and loop fasteners: strips or squares
- Sequins, paint, string, stickers to decorate the chests

What to do:

1. Talk with the children about treasure boxes – what they look like and who has them. Remind them about pirate treasure chests and tell a pirate story.

2. Show the children how to cut the cereal boxes, and let them cut them to make a box and curved lid (see photo). You can draw the lines for them to cut if you think they need this support.

3. Cover your treasure chests with scrunched-up silver foil.

4. Decorate the chest with string handles, a 'lock', straps and other special things.

5. Fasten your box with a 'sticky fixer'.

6. Fill the boxes with personal treasures, or collect unwanted beads and other jewellery from charity shops.

7. Make telescopes from cardboard tubes, eye patches from black card, and find some red bandanas for headbands. Now turn your climbing frame into a pirate ship and sail away!

Top tip ⭐

Stuff the box with screwed-up newspaper to make it firmer to work on.

Taking it forward

- Make another box and use it as a story box, with objects linked to your current story.
- Suggest that the children take their boxes home for their own special treasures.

What's in it for the children?

Having a place to keep their own special treasures is important for young children's sense of self.

Captured

A simple ship in a bottle

What you need:

- A real ship in a bottle, or some photos of one
- Some empty water bottles (large, medium and small)
- Blue or green playdough
- Thick polystyrene (to cut into simple boat hull shapes)
- Hot wire or craft knife (adult use only)
- Card, paper, cocktail sticks, garden sticks, cotton
- Glue, scissors, felt pens

Top tip ⭐

Put a line of masking tape round the bottle where you want to cut, and cut through the tape and bottle together. This will stop it from splitting.

Taking it forward

- Download some 'Pirates of the Caribbean' photos from the internet and use them as a background for a display of your ships in bottles.
- Write stories about pirates and treasure ships.

What's in it for the children?

Making a replica of something an adult can do is very good for self-image and confidence.

 Health & Safety
Take care with anything hot or sharp.

What to do:

1. Prepare the resources and cut some polystyrene hull shapes about 8–10 cm long, using a hot wire or sharp knife. The children can watch from a safe distance.

2. Now show the children the ship in a bottle and talk about how the ship gets in there! You could find some pictures on the internet.

3. Tell the children that you will show them how to make a ship in a bottle, but because it's such a fiddly job to do a real one, this is an easy way!

4. Take a water bottle and put a line of tape round it near the bottom end. Cut along the end and carefully remove the bottom of the bottle – this is the trick! Keep each bottle and bottom together.

5. Now talk about making boats to fit in the bottles. The children will need to work to a small scale, and some will not be able to make something small enough to go in an individual water bottle. They will need something bigger – a litre bottle or a juice bottle may work.

6. Help the children to fix the masts and other features on to their boats, making suggestions but not taking over.

7. Put the bottles on their sides and put some blue or green playdough in the bottom to represent the sea. Use a cocktail stick or pen to make wave shapes.

8. Gently press the completed ships onto the 'sea' in the bottles, and when the children are happy with their own ship, carefully stick the end of the bottle back with tape.

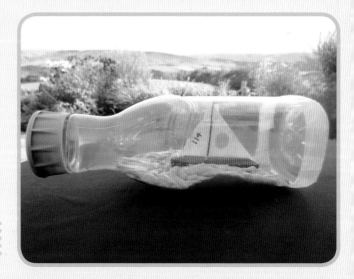

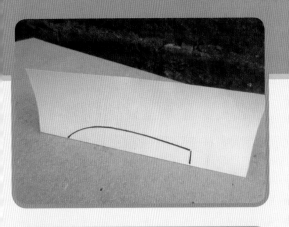

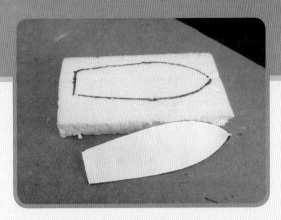

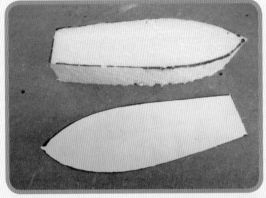

Fire! Fire!
Make paint balloons

Top tip ⭐
Use washing-up liquid bottles to help get the paint and water into the balloons.

What you need:

- Big sheets of strong paper or card
- Balloons
- Ready-mixed paint, thinned
- Water
- Masking tape
- A sharp needle (adult supervised)

What to do:

1. Put some big sheets of paper on the floor, preferably outside. Weigh them down with bricks or stones.

2. Talk with the children about what you are going to do, and remind them that they should only squirt paint at the paper and not at other people.

3. Give each child an empty balloon to hold and put some paint in each one: about three tablespoons in each will do.

4. Top up the balloon with water, using another bottle or a jug and funnel.

5. Help the children to tie the balloons and show them how to swirl them around to mix the paint and water.

6. Put a piece of tape on each balloon, at the opposite end from the fastening. This will stop the balloon from bursting when you push the needle into it.

7. Gently push a needle into the balloon through the tape (adult use only).

8. Now get squirting by squeezing the balloon to fire paint at the big sheets of paper.

Taking it forward

- Put more than one hole in each balloon – you will need to work very quickly!
- Try squirting paint on paper fixed to the wall or fence (outside).

What's in it for the children?

This activity is a combination of control and chaos. Children need to experience both!

 Health & Safety

Ensure the children are clear that needles are for adults only.

Sand socks

Slapping paint–covered socks

What you need:

- Old socks – thin adult socks are easier to tie
- Sand and a scoop
- Elastic bands
- Several colours of paint in shallow bowls
- An old sheet
- A climbing frame or other safe platform above the ground

What to do:

1. Spread the sheet on the ground by the climbing frame, and hold it down with bricks or stones.
2. Put the paint bowls on the ground near the sheet.
3. Let the children help to scoop some sand into each sock and tie the end in a knot, or fix it with a strong elastic band.
4. Dip the sand sock in the paint and slap it on the sheet to make a painty mark. Change colours.
5. Climb the climbing frame with a sand sock and drop it onto the sheet from a height. What happens?
6. When the children have finished let the picture dry and use it as a table cover, curtain or screen.

Taking it forward

- Dip the sand socks in water before dipping in dry paint powder. What happens to the patterns now?
- Fill socks with pea gravel, marbles or used paper towels. Drop them from a height and see what happens to the socks when they have different things inside them.

What's in it for the children?

It's important for children to experiment with familiar materials in a more structured activity, where they can compare and contrast different responses.

 Health & Safety

Make sure the children know not to throw any objects at each other, even in fun.

Top tip ⭐

Cut the feet off old tights as well as using socks.

Assault course

Make an obstacle race with all your outdoor equipment

What you need:

- Playground chalk
- Any outdoor climbing equipment, fixed or moveable
- Blankets and drapes
- Tunnels
- Big cardboard boxes
- Cones, baskets, balls
- A silver foil survival blanket
- Ropes
- Hoops
- Anything else in your cupboard or shed!

 **Health & Safety**

Use masking tape to secure slippery things such as hoops.

What to do:

1. Talk to the children about making an assault course. Find out if any of them have been on an activity course at a theme park or adventure playground, and encourage them to tell you about it.

2. Go outside and look at all the things you could use.

3. Draw a chalk line where the children think the course should go, not forgetting to include the fixed equipment.

4. Now start putting out the equipment along the line, joining larger pieces with skipping ropes, chalk footsteps, planks or beanbags.

5. Use tunnels, blankets and drapes for crawling under, and cut the ends out of big boxes to crawl through.

6. Put little challenges at some points, such as bouncing a ball into a bucket, skipping six times, climbing to the top of the climbing frame and coming down the slide, or weaving in and out of cones. The children will think of lots of things to do, so make sure you incorporate their ideas.

7. Put a basket of dressing-up clothes half way round so they can put something funny on for the rest of the challenge.

8. Practice the assault course so everyone knows how to do it, then let the children manage it themselves, as you watch from a distance.

Top tip ⭐

Get some big clothes such as adult T-shirts, pyjama bottoms, ballet tutus, hats and sunglasses to put on as the children go round.

50 fantastic ideas to captivate boys

Taking it forward

■ You can do these challenges in all seasons. Winter courses need to be different but they can be just as much fun, using equipment differently, with less crawling and more running and jumping.

What's in it for the children?

Making an assault course and using it will develop imagination and creativity as well as exercising muscles.

Strike!
Make your own bowling game

What you need:

- Empty plastic milk, juice or laundry liquid bottles with tops
- Sand or gravel
- A plastic funnel
- Three tennis balls
- Permanent marker or black duct tape
- Stickers (optional)
- Chalk or a playground spray marker

Top tip

Self-adhesive numbers, coloured adhesive tape or stickers will make your pins look extra smart and professional.

Taking it forward

- Add more sand to the pins, to make them more difficult to knock over.
- Offer some clipboards and pens for scoring, or set up some more lanes and make more pins for a tournament.

What's in it for the children?

Games with aiming and throwing improve hand-eye co-ordination. They also help children to get used to winning and losing. Scoring will help with number skills.

 Health & Safety

Always use soft balls for throwing games, and locate your bowling lanes against a wall or fence.

What to do:

1. Remove all the labels and plastic covering from the bottles.
2. Make sure the bottles and the tops are clean and absolutely dry inside.
3. Explain that you are making a bowling game, and let the children help.
4. Using the funnel, fill the bottles with equal amounts of sand, either by counting scoops or by measuring the level in each bottle. Start with the bottles being about one third full.
5. Put a top on each bottle and screw it on tightly. These bottles are the 'pins'.
6. Look together for a good place for a bowling lane, with a fence or wall at the end.
7. Use chalk or spray to mark out a bowling lane, and crosses or dots to show where to place the pins. You may need several bowling lanes for children of different ages.
8. Set up your pins.
9. Take three balls and get bowling!

50 fantastic ideas to captivate boys

Down the tubes

Make a marble run

What you need:

- Lots of cardboard tubes of all lengths and diameters
- Masking tape
- Duct tape
- Scissors
- Children's saws
- Bricks and boxes to support the run
- Marbles or small balls

Top tip ⭐

Get marbles, plastic balls or small rubber bouncey balls from bargain or 'pound' shops.

Taking it forward

- Try rolling some different objects down the run – toy cars, pebbles, beads of different sizes, other balls or coins. Which work best? Why?

- Use a timer or stopwatch to time different objects or different sorts of marbles. Try guessing the timings first to see how well you can estimate.

What's in it for the children?

Working in a group to make something together is very good for social development. Evaluating a structure and making alterations is a difficult but useful skill to foster.

Health & Safety

Supervise the use of woodwork tools, even those sold especially for children.

What to do:

1. Involve children and their families in collecting as many tubes as you can:
   - from kitchen roll, foil, wrapping paper and cling film
   - from fabric rolls (try shops and market traders)
   - from carpets (ask your local carpet shop or DIY store)
   - sections of old garden hose
   - drainpipes and guttering.

2. When you have a good selection, talk with the children about how to make a marble or ball run.

3. Help the children to make the run, building sections and testing them.

4. Make suggestions for supporting the run and making the joints smooth so the marbles or balls don't stop in the middle. Take some photos of the process.

5. Encourage the children to experiment with their run. Explain that sometimes it's better to take something apart and build it again if it doesn't work well.

6. When the run is finished the children could decorate it with stickers and flags.

Dinosaur roar
A dinosaur story box

What you need:

- Shoeboxes with lids
- Tape
- Scissors
- Craft knife (adult use only)
- Newspaper
- Wallpaper paste or diluted white glue
- Paints and brushes
- Silver foil, playdough
- Natural objects: stones, sand, gravel, moss, sticks and small branches
- Small world dinosaurs

Top tip ⭐

Make your own paste from a cup of flour and half a cup of water.

Taking it forward

- Make some other story boxes from shoeboxes or bigger cardboard boxes, for other small world figures or sets.
- Help children to make photo stories using their story boxes.

What's in it for the children?

This activity gives children plenty of opportunities to use their imagination and creativity alone or in small groups.

 Health & Safety

Make it clear that craft knives must only be used by adults.

What to do:

1. Look at the boxes and think about how they could be made into dinosaur worlds.

2. To make the shoebox into a story box, cut down two corners of the box. This makes more playing space, and the flap closes when the lid is replaced, making a secure and easily stored resource.

3. Talk about how the box could be decorated, inside and outside, to make a dinosaur scene. Think about the back and sides of the inside of the box and what you might see there – sky, clouds, trees, volcanoes, flying dinosaurs! Some children may like to draw these on paper and stick them in the box, or you could paint them directly onto the box.

4. Look at the flat floor of the box and think about what might be there – a pond made from silver foil, sand paths, rocks, hills made from scrunched newspaper covered with pasted strips, trees made from sticks standing in playdough.

5. Cover and decorate the outside of the box, and the lid.

6. Help the children to make their own worlds in their story boxes. When they have finished, use the boxes for storytelling or imaginative small world play.

7. If you 'theme' the box and the lid, it will be easy for children to find which story box they want to play with.

Make it fly!

Simple planes from polystyrene trays

What you need:

- Clean, flat polystyrene food trays
- Scissors
- Pencils
- Fine permanent markers, stickers or coloured tape
- Sticky tack or paper clips
- Card or extra polystyrene for templates

Taking it forward

- Have a flying contest to see whose plane flies best.
- Try making planes from other recycled materials, or from balsa wood, which is easy to work with.

What's in it for the children?

This activity is quick to do, and gives children a sense of independence as they can do most of it on their own.

What to do:

1. Cut the bottoms out of the polystyrene trays, so you have flat rectangular pieces.
2. Use the illustrations and your prototype to make some templates for the planes from card or polystyrene.
3. Show the children the materials for plane making and the completed plane you have made.
4. Now the children can make their own plane by drawing around the templates onto the polystyrene with a pen, to make the three pieces of the plane (wings, body and tail).
5. Help the children to cut slots for the wings and tail.
6. It's easier to decorate the wings and fuselage with stickers or tape before you fit them together (not too many, or the plane will be too heavy to fly!).
7. Fit the wings and tail by pushing them through the slots.
8. Fix some sticky tack on a paperclip to the nose of the plane (see photograph).
9. Test the planes. These little planes should fly well, but don't throw too hard!
10. Provide plenty of polystyrene to make replacements, as the planes are quite fragile.

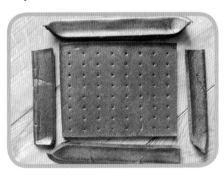

> ### Top tip ⭐
> Make an example of the plane yourself first, so you can check how it works!

> ### ➕ Health & Safety
> Always wash food trays thoroughly, preferably in a dishwasher, before providing them for children to use.

Frozen cubes
Make big ice cubes to paint with

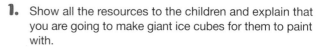

What you need:

- Access to a freezer
- Plastic containers of all shapes:
  - plastic beakers and milk bottles
  - yogurt pots and plastic food containers
  - plastic cups
  - small plastic bowls
- Scissors
- Water
- Ready-mixed paint in several colours
- Wooden lolly sticks or plastic spoons
- Cling film
- Big sheets of strong paper or card
- Masking tape

What to do:

1. Show all the resources to the children and explain that you are going to make giant ice cubes for them to paint with.

2. Let each child choose a container and fill it with a mixture of paint and water. Use plenty of paint.

3. Cover the containers tightly with cling film. Some containers may need a bit of tape or an elastic band to keep the cling film tight.

4. Now make two or three small holes in the cling film with scissors and poke sticks or spoons into the water. The cling film should hold the sticks up.

5. Put the containers in a freezer.

6. When the containers are frozen, tape some strong paper over a table.

7. Dip the frozen containers briefly in a bowl of warm water to release the ice, and slip them onto the paper.

8. Move the ice shapes around using the stick handles to make a melting ice pattern.

9. Change the paper regularly or it may disintegrate.

Taking it forward

- Make some giant cubes in ice cream tubs, baking tins or plastic trays, with six or more sticks in them. Use these outside to 'paint' the patio.

- Make tiny cubes with really strong paint in ice cube trays or bun tins for little pictures.

What's in it for the children?

Exploring ice will give children experience of changing materials by freezing and melting.

Top tip ⭐

Cut the tops from juice cartons, milk bottles or other containers with straight sides and use the bottoms for this activity.

The human pendulum
An artistic use for a swing

What you need:

- A tyre swing or a swing with a seat
- Big felt pens or paintbrushes and thick paint
- A big sheet of thick card
- Big sheets of paper
- Tape, stones or big bricks

Top tip ⭐

A low swing fixed from one point, such as a tyre, is best because it swings in all directions, giving a more complicated effect. Get an old tyre from your local tyre dealer.

Taking it forward

- Use paintbrushes with water, or chalks on the ground, instead of markers.

- Try it with the human pendulum moving their arms as they swing, and then with them keeping them still. Look at the differences.

- Try it with food colouring and water in small hand sprays on an old sheet, to make a unique curtain or divider for your room or outdoor area.

What's in it for the children?

Swinging has been proven to stimulate children's brains. Perhaps that's why they like it so much!

➕ Health & Safety

Supervise this activity, and watch carefully to avoid children falling or observers bumping into the swing.

What to do:

1. Put the card on the ground under the swing to create a smooth surface.

2. Put a sheet of paper on the card and hold it down at the corners with stones, bricks or tape.

3. Make a chalk or rope circle round the swing to protect observers.

4. Explain how the children can be human pendulums by lying face down on the swing with a thick marker in each hand.

5. Gently push the swing so the human pendulum can make patterns on the paper with the pens.

6. Experiment with different speeds, arm positions and directions.

7. Once the children are used to the experience, let them try with their eyes shut, or even with a blindfold.

8. Change the paper for the next human pendulum to have a turn.

Growing den

Making living dens and shelters

What you need:

- A sheet, cheap shower curtain or a decorators' plastic dust sheet
- Garden canes or long sticks
- Hammer or mallet
- Cable ties and bulldog clips
- Masking tape
- Thin rope or thick string
- Runner bean seeds
- Trowels

What to do:

1. Collect all the things you need and discuss them with the children. Explain that they are going to make a den that is also a garden! Talk about the seeds and look at the pictures on the packet.

2. Start by together choosing a place for the den.

3. Help the children to hammer the sticks firmly in the ground in a 'wigwam' shape, making it as big and as firm as possible. Tie the sticks at the top.

4. If you haven't got a lawn, just tie the sticks at the top and they should stay up.

5. Cover the den with a sheet of fabric or plastic, fixing it with cable ties and clips so it won't blow away. You can make a door flap or leave the doorway open.

6. Put an old piece of carpet or a groundsheet in your den.

7. Now dig holes on the outside of the den at the bottom of each stick or pole, and plant three bean seeds in each hole. Don't forget to water them, and they should grow quickly, particularly if you plant them in the spring or early summer.

8. If you are working on a hard surface, stand the den 'legs' in plant pots of compost for the beans to grow in.

Top tip ★

Longer sticks make bigger dens. Look at the options in your local garden centre.

Taking it forward

- Some other plants that could grow up your living den are: nasturtiums, mile-a-minute vine, honeysuckle and other climbers. Choose ones that have either fruit or flowers. A good garden centre will help you to choose, especially if you take the children with you.

- Plant a living willow wigwam in your setting for a permanent shelter.

What's in it for the children?

Building a den together uses many skills, both physical and social.

✚ Health & Safety

Watch for splinters, especially in bamboo canes.

The box room

Make a secret room from a very big carton

What you need:

- **Very big cartons** (those from household appliances such as fridges or washing machines are ideal)
- **Masking and duct tape**
- **Craft knife** (adult use only)
- **Scissors**
- **Markers**
- **Emulsion paint**
- **Decorators' brushes**

Top tip ★

Use up those old tins of emulsion paint from your garage, but make sure the paint is water based!

Taking it forward

- You may want to discuss rules for the secret room, such as how many children can go inside at once, or how the adults can check that children are safe.

- If you don't want an enclosed secret room, cut the top or front off the box so you can see what is going on inside. You can cover the roof with a removable drape, a net curtain or a clear shower curtain.

What's in it for the children?

Planning and making their own room is a task that needs many skills, social and interpersonal as well as physical.

Health & Safety

Make it clear that using a craft knife is an activity for adults only.

What to do:

1. Show the children the big carton and tell them they are going to make it into a secret room, just for themselves.

2. Talk about how they could make it secret. Offer your suggestions, but don't ignore theirs!

3. Tape the box up entirely, on all sides, with duct tape.

4. Ask the children to draw on the box where they want the door to be. If the room is only for children, help them to make the door just big enough for them. It could be a round or square doorway, with a hinged door or a curtain.

5. Do they want any windows? You can make opening windows by drawing an 'H' shape on its side, cutting along the lines, and bending back the two windows. Cut finger holes for opening and shutting.

6. Let the children decide if they want to paint or decorate their house, outside or inside or both. Emulsion paint will make it wtaerproof against showers (though not heavy rain), for use outdoors.

7. The children can decide whether they want any furniture, cushions, or other objects inside.

A den for my hero

Making a den from fabric for a small toy

Top tip ⭐

Ask parents if they are willing to supply unwanted scarves and saris for the children to use.

What you need:

- Favourite small world characters, superheroes or TV/DVD characters from home
- Thin fabric such as sheeting, sari fabric, scarves, old shirts
- Paint pots or bowls, and brushes
- White glue mixed with water (50/50)
- Plastic carrier bags
- Scissors, secateurs (optional/ adult use only)
- Short garden sticks or thin canes
- Cable ties or string
- Clothes pegs

What to do:

1. Work with small groups on this activity, until children are confident, then they can go on without you.

2. Show the children how to make a small wigwam shape with four or six sticks. Cut longer sticks with secateurs (adults only).

3. Fix the sticks at the top with a cable tie or string, and check that the den is big enough for the toy.

4. Now show the children how to estimate how much fabric they will need to cover their den by wrapping it round the sticks and cutting off any extra. Some children will need help here.

5. Show how to spread out a plastic carrier bag and spread the fabric on the plastic.

6. Cover the fabric completely with white glue/water mix.

7. Carefully lift the fabric and drape it over the den. Don't worry if isn't big enough, just add more gluey fabric. If it's too big you can trim it later. Hold the fabric with clothes pegs if you need to.

8. Leave to dry. The fabric will stiffen and children will be able to trim off any spare bits with scissors.

9. Decorate the dens with felt pens or paint.

✚ Health & Safety

Warn children to be careful when working with sticks.

Taking it forward

- Use this technique to make hanging pictures. Tie three or four sticks together at the corners and cover the square or triangle with gluey tissue paper on one side. Put the picture flat, add some sequins, shapes or a picture of your favourite superhero, and cover with another sheet of gluey tissue. Hang from a string. The tissue will become transparent as it dries.

What's in it for the children?

Learning how things change as they dry is good early science.

Dark, but not dangerous
Painting blindfold

What you need:

- A painting easel or paper pinned to a wall or fence
- Thick paint in non-spill pots
- Brushes
- Soft scarves for blindfolds
- Aprons
- Plastic floor covering or newspaper

What to do:

1. This is a good activity for a topic on 'My five senses' or 'My body'. Talk to the children about the blindfold game, and explain how switching off one of your senses makes you use the other senses more.

2. Help the children to make some very thick paint by adding cornflour or paste.

3. Sit by the easel, and show the children the blindfold. Put it on yourself, and have a go at painting a picture, so the children know what to do.

4. Now ask for a volunteer to have the next turn.

5. The volunteer should stand in front of the easel with the blindfold on, and paint a picture without seeing what they are doing. They can decide the point at which they have finished their picture.

6. Ask the first child to tell you all what it was like painting without being able to see.

7. Change the paper for another child, and leave the activity for free choice, preferably for pairs of friends. Make sure you revisit the children regularly to talk and support them.

Top tip ★

Keep your eye masks from holiday flights - they make great blindfolds.

Taking it forward

- Try doing other things with a blindfold on: washing your hands, brick building, or finger painting.

- Try 'switching off' another sense – wearing big earphones, doing something with thick gloves on, or holding your nose and trying to smell things.

What's in it for the children?

Children need to appreciate their own senses and how it feels to be without sight – relying on their other senses.

 ### Health & Safety

Some children may be scared by or unsure of this activity. Never force them to join in, just let them watch.

Find it!

A scavenger hunt

What you need:

- Paper or plastic collecting bags, one between two
- Scavenger hunt lists – enough for one between two children
- Pencils

Top tip

Pair the children so that there is one reader in the pair, or make a pictorial list.

✚ Health & Safety

If you do your scavenger hunt at the park or in the woods, warn children to be careful about what they pick up.

What to do:

1. Make your scavenger hunt lists and stick them on the bags. Picture clues really help!

2. Ask the children if they have ever been on a scavenger hunt before. Explain that it is different from a treasure hunt, because there are no clues, just a list of things to collect. Every time they find an object they tick it off the list.

3. Read the scavenger hunt list together, and make sure everyone understands what to do.

4. Give the children time to collect the objects – about five minutes is fine to start with.

5. When the children get back, sit together and let the children spread their finds out on the floor to talk about.

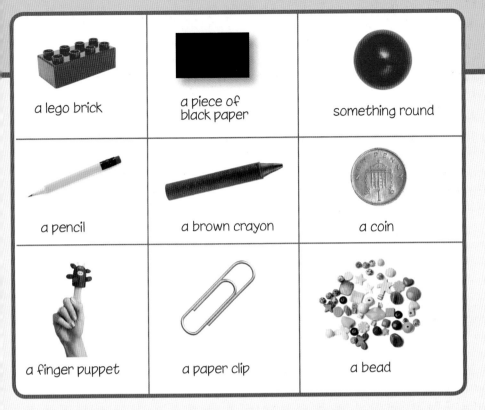

a lego brick	a piece of black paper	something round
a pencil	a brown crayon	a coin
a finger puppet	a paper clip	a bead

Taking it forward

- Make the scavenger hunts more difficult as children get used to them. Do hunts in different seasons and different weather. Here is a sample list that you could use on a walk:

- Something fuzzy
- A seed
- A flower
- Something straight
- Something round
- Something smooth
- Something rough
- Two different leaves

- Something that makes a noise
- A chewed leaf
- A beautiful rock
- A pinecone
- Something green
- A stick
- A treasure

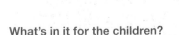

What's in it for the children?

This activity needs co-operation and concentration in pairs, particularly as the scavenger hunts get more difficult.

Let's be brickies

Making bricks with mud

What you need:

- A couple of real bricks (as examples)
- Digging tools
- Mud, potting soil or compost
- White glue
- Buckets or bowls
- Water
- As many unwanted ice cube trays as you can collect

Top tip ⭐

Ask around to see if you can find someone who can supply some soil with high clay content. Mix some of this soil with compost to help it stick together.

Taking it forward

- Use small pieces of plywood or thick card for a base.
- Add small world people, wood off-cuts and garden finds such as twigs, leaves, stones and grass to make your buildings more realistic.

What's in it for the children?

Using a real process on a small scale is a good way for children to find out about the world.

✚ Health & Safety

Wash your hands when you have finished working, and make sure the children don't eat the mud!

What to do:

1. Show the children the resources and suggest that they could make some bricks for building. Look at real bricks together and explain how they are made from clay from under the ground.

2. If you have a garden or digging area, the children could dig up their own soil and use that for an even more realistic experience.

3. Mix the soil and break up the lumps in some buckets, using trowels or forks. Remove any stones.

4. Squidge the soil in your hands and see if it sticks together easily. You may need to add some water, white glue or sand. Experiment to see how much you need. Aim for the consistency of soft ice-cream.

5. Lightly oil the ice cube trays to make it easier to pop out the dry bricks.

6. When the mud seems the right consistency, press it into the ice cube trays, using a pencil end to tamp it down. Smooth the tops with a wet spoon or butter knife.

7. Leave your bricks in the warmest place you can find (not the oven) for at least 24 hours (over a weekend is even better), until they are hard.

8. Gently tip the bricks out and you are ready to build.

9. Use liquid mud (mud with some water and a bit of white glue) to stick the bricks together.

10. Look at the bricks as you work, and see if you need to adjust your recipe before you make some more.

Air painting challenge

Painting something with one hand

What you need:

- A light football or beach ball
- String
- White paper
- Masking tape
- Scissors
- Ground sheet or opened-out bin-liner

Top tip ⭐

A light ball is best, as it moves more.

Taking it forward

- Wrap other shapes in paper for air painting: try small boxes, shoes, a cucumber or even a pineapple.
- Open an old umbrella, hang it up and decorate it with paint — or cut the fabric off and hang things from the ribs to make a mobile.

What's in it for the children?

The challenge of using one hand really makes children concentrate.

 Health & Safety

Make sure the ball is securely fixed to the ceiling or a climbing frame.

What to do:

1. Tie the string round the ball, leaving enough hanging to suspend the ball from the ceiling or a climbing frame. You will probably need to tape it in place. Don't hang it up yet!

2. Wrap the paper around the ball in a cylinder. Then fold and press the ends of the paper in and tape them so the paper completely covers the ball.

3. Hang the ball securely from the ceiling, or from a climbing frame if you are outdoors so it is at eye level for the children. Position a large ground sheet below it.

4. Now challenge the children to paint the ball, using one hand only. They must not touch the ball with their other hand.

5. When the ball is covered and the paint is dry – this may involve several children – you can leave it hanging as a decoration.

6. Alternatively, you could take the ball down and unwrap it, smooth out the painting and display it. Talk about why the paint is not all over the paper.

7. Wrap the ball again for another creation. This time, hang it slightly higher, or slightly lower.

Can you hear me?

Make sound tubes and telephones

What you need:

- Empty tin cans or yogurt pots
- Hammer and a big nail
- String
- Scissors

or

- Plastic tubing or old garden hose (any length, but try 3 or 4 meters)
- Small plastic funnels
- Duct tape

What to do:

1. Collect all the things you need and talk with the children about making telephones. Show them both ways of making them.

2. The first way is traditional: make small holes in the bottoms of two empty cans or yogurt pots, using scissors (yoghurt pots) or a hammer and a big nail (cans). Thread string through the holes and knot inside the can or pot. Stretch the string until it is tight. If using a yoghurt pot, tie the string to a matchstick and fix it with a blob of glue. This will stop it pulling out if the string is drawn tight. One child speaks in their end; the other listens, then replies.

3. The second way works better over distances: fix the funnels to the two ends of a length of tube. Cover the join with duct tape. Children take a funnel each, and walk away as far as they can, then they take turns to talk and listen through the funnels. See how quietly you can talk and still be heard. This method will also work from the top to the bottom of a slide or a climbing frame, under blankets or around corners.

Top tip ⭐

Get small plastic funnels from bargain or 'pound' shops, and plastic tubing from an aquarium supplier.

Taking it forward

- Get some old mobile phones and take out the batteries before using them in free play.

- Talk about the difference between phone calls, text messages and email. Practice sending some emails to each other on your computer.

What's in it for the children?

Simple experiments with sounds can lead to more complex scientific investigations.

Health & Safety

Warn the children about the tripping hazards of long strings and tubing.

Boys on film

Make a PowerPoint presentation to show to other children

What you need:

- A digital camera
- An empty water or sand tray
- Access to:
  - collections of small world figures and objects (superheroes, animals, underwater, spacemen, knights, etc.)
  - boxes
  - rocks, stones, sand, gravel
  - natural objects like moss, leaves and twigs
  - fabrics, colored card and paper, pens

What to do:

1. Before the session, make sure the resources are easily accessible, so the children can start at once.

2. Talk with a group about making a PowerPoint story to show on your whiteboard or computer.

3. If the children know how to use cameras, they will be able to start thinking immediately. If they have never done this before, they may need the full support of an adult.

4. Help the children to decide what their story is going to be about, and also assist where necessary in collecting the small world and other resources they need.

5. Agree who will be the camera operator, and agree a word (such as 'freeze') for when s/he is going to take a shot.

6. Continue with the story or sequence of actions, talking about what will happen next, looking at the photo sequence so far, deciding when to change the story, and when the story is finished.

7. Look at the photo sequence on the camera, download the photos to a computer and import them into PowerPoint.

8. Help the children to write captions for the pictures. Run the whole sequence to check that it is right.

9. Now get an audience to watch your story, as one member of the group reads the captions.

Taking it forward

- As the children get more familiar with using cameras, they will be able to make more complex presentations or photo books.

- Get some background pictures to inspire stories: wrapping paper, fabrics, the backings for aquariums, or photos from the internet. Mount these pictures on card to put behind the small world characters.

What's in it for the children?

Storytelling is more difficult for some children if they think they have to write it down. Practical ways of storytelling will give all children confidence.

Health & Safety

Always teach children how to use electronic equipment safely.

Outside sounds

Sounds and music in the garden

What you need:

- Old saucepans and lids, metal teapots and kettles
- Old metal cutlery
- Pieces of metal tubing
- Camping plates and mugs
- Clean, empty tin cans
- Bells of all sizes
- Bottle tops
- String
- Wooden spoons and sticks

What to do:

1. If you have a wooden or chain link fence, you can hang the music makers directly on it. Otherwise you will need to put up some brackets or wooden battens in a corner where children can work without being interrupted by other activities.

2. Offer other simple instruments such as chopsticks, kazoos, mouth organs, maracas, tambourines and wrist bells.

3. Encourage children to make their own instruments and beaters from the materials you've collected.

4. Show them how to make drums by stretching plastic from carrier bags over clean biscuit tins. Tape or tie the plastic tightly and play with chopsticks or sticks with wadded fabric fixed to the ends using elastic bands.

5. Offer a radio or CD player so they can sing along as they make music to their favourite tunes.

6. Sometimes go out as a whole group and have a singing or music session outside.

7. Have a parade every so often, with flags, banners and singing.

Top tip ⭐

Make some shakers with gravel, sand and stones in empty plastic bottles.

Taking it forward

- Build a stage in your music corner, so the children can stage informal concerts or karaoke sessions.

- Add some wind chimes, bells and strings of shells hung from branches or guttering, or get some cheap plastic bowls to use upside down for drumming.

What's in it for the children?

Making this sort of music supports the development of rhythm, timing, beat and pitch, all essential for learning to read and write.

✚ Health & Safety

Check the objects regularly and remove any that are rusty or have sharp edges.

Make it move!

Make a waterway on a fence

Top tip ★

Guttering and drainpipes are often available from recycling centres and scrap stores.

What you need:

- Short pieces of plastic guttering and drainpipes, guttering clips
- String and thin rope
- Duct tape
- Elastic 'bungees' (from car shops)
- Plastic bottles and boxes, buckets and bowls
- Funnels
- Screws, screwdrivers, hammers, nails
- A small cordless electric drill (optional)

Taking it forward

- Make the waterway go even further, propping it up if necessary and adding new resources as they get used. Link it to climbing frames, trees, and other parts of your garden or play area.
- Link downpipes and gutters on the building to your waterway, watch what happens when it rains, and then link everything to the drains.
- Offer food colouring to check where the water is going.

What's in it for the children?

Solving practical problems keeps young brains working and growing. The sense of achievement on completing the challenge will be significant.

✚ Health & Safety

Young children can use electric drills under good supervision, but they must be trained in their safety and always work one-to-one with an adult.

What to do:

1. Go outside together and look at the fence. Show children the tools and resources, and challenge them to build a waterway to take water from one end of the fence to the other.

2. Make sure they know how to use the tools safely, and then stay around to provide help if needed, and to take photos as the project progresses.

3. Help them to use the guttering and containers by nailing or screwing them to the fence or using brackets.

4. Suggest that they test their waterway regularly to make sure it's working, adding new features and changing things that don't work so well.

Come to our barbecue!

Hold a barbecue in your setting

What you need:

- A disposable or portable barbecue
- Some tape or barriers to fence off the barbecue area
- Wooden barbecue skewers
- Chipolata sausages, mince for burgers (plus vegetarian options)
- Small burger buns and hot dog buns
- Ketchup and other condiments
- Plenty of paper plates, cups and napkins
- Drinks

Top tip ⭐

Have your barbecue at the end of the day and invite the parents to come too.

What to do:

1. Talk to the children and ask them if they would like to invite their parents to a barbecue. They will surely say yes!

2. You will need to plan the event, talk to your managers, write letters to the parents, organise your outside area, shop for and prepare the food. The children can help with all of these. They can write invitations (or at least sign and decorate a photocopied invitation).

3. Children can help to organise your garden so it is tidy and attractive, with plenty of places for parents to sit, and safe places for toddlers and babies to play.

4. If you can, involve children in shopping for ingredients. Let them help to make burgers, dilute squash in jugs, cut buns in half, put out crisps or other snacks. They can make signs and labels for the area, prepare rubbish bins, decorate the garden with flags or balloons, and choose some music.

5. During the barbecue, children can be waiters taking the food and drinks round. They can take photos, play with the little children, and even sing or dance for the parents.

6. And at the end they can help you to clear up and put things back where they belong!

Taking it forward

- This could start a series of events for parents. You could consider a 'Dads and lads' day, a bulb planting session, a coffee morning to make things for the Christmas fair or a sewing session to make dressing up and dolls' clothes.

What's in it for the children?

Entertaining their families is a special event in children's lives. When we give them a chance to host, they often exceed our expectations.

✚ Health & Safety

Make sure the barbecue is safely managed while it is alight, and put out properly at the end of the session. Before you start, check for food allergies.

50 fantastic ideas to captivate boys

Ring around
Make and play quoits

What you need:

- Garden hose or thick rope
- Duct tape
- Plastic water or milk bottles
- Food colouring or paint
- Sand
- Permanent markers

Top tip ⭐

You could set some sticks in plaster or plastercine in plant pots to make different sorts of posts.

Taking it forward

- Make the game more difficult by standing the bottles in a line, one behind the other.

- Write numbers on the bottles and record your scores.

What's in it for the children?

Making and playing your own game is a very satisfying activity. Scoring is good for number skills.

✚ Health & Safety

Throwing games should always be set up in front of a fence or wall.

What to do:

1. Cut the rope into lengths about 40cm long. You may need to experiment with the length to make a suitable ring – some lengths of rope and hosepipe are quite stiff.

2. Tape the ends securely together with duct tape to form a ring.

3. Make lots of these. The children can help by holding the ends together for you to tape, or they may be able to help each other in pairs.

4. Half fill the water bottles with dry sand. Top up with water and add some food colouring or paint, a different colour in each.

5. Fix the tops securely, using tape if necessary. Now you are ready to play quoits!

6. Arrange the bottles in a circle, and draw a chalk line on the ground a little way away.

7. Stand on the line to throw. Take turns to throw two, three or five quoits over the bottles.

8. Vary the game by throwing from further away, standing on one leg, throwing with a different hand, or even throwing with your eyes closed.

Are we there yet?

Set up an endless roadway

What you need:

- Lots of empty cereal packets
- Masking tape
- Scissors
- Felt pens

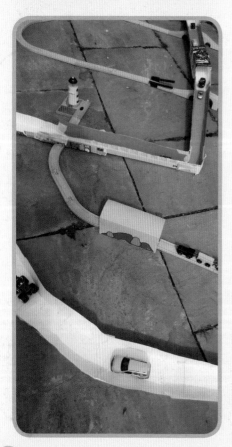

What to do:

1. Sit with the children and tell them you are all going to make an endless roadway for their toy cars.

2. Once you have shown them the principle of the activity, a group of children can work totally independently.

3. For the first box, you could draw cutting lines for the children to follow. Show them how to use scissors to score the cardboard, to make folding easier. After this they should be able to do the rest on their own.

4. Use scissors to cut the boxes about 5 cm from each edge (see photos of track). You should be able to get four pieces of 'track' out of each packet.

5. Stick the pieces together to form the car track.

6. When the track reaches an obstacle, the children will need to solve the problem of going round corners or over things.

7. To go round corners, show them how to cut a shape like a pizza slice from the leftover card and use this to join two pieces — one along the long edge, and one along the top of the 'slice'. Cut a guardrail and stick this with tape round the curve.

8. To go over obstacles, use big wooden bricks to support the track.

9. Of course, going under obstacles will be easy and fun!

10. Use smaller boxes and tubes to make tunnels.

11. Try the track with cars and adjust it to make the cars go faster.

12. Extend the track to go both outside and indoors.

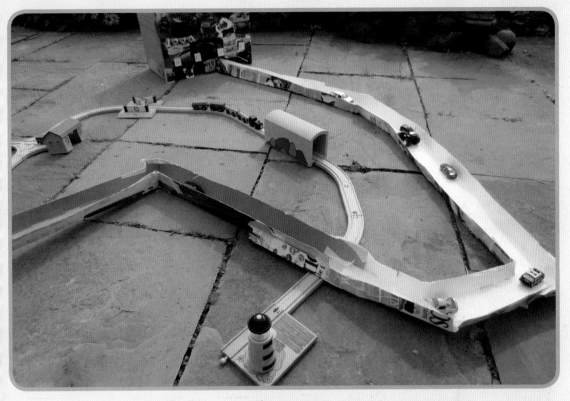

Top tip ⭐

Use the sides of the boxes too!

Taking it forward

- Find more boxes to make a petrol station, car park or shops.

- Make the track waterproof by painting it with PVA, covering it with sticky-backed plastic, or shielding it under lengths of upside down guttering.

What's in it for the children?

An ongoing project that is made entirely by themselves will engage most boys, even though individuals in the group may change.

Spinning

The excitement of a salad spinner

What you need:

- A plastic salad spinner or two
- Paper
- Paint and small spoons
- Glitter or confetti
- Scissors

What to do:

1. Cut some paper circles to fit the bottom of the salad spinner.

2. Put paint in some small containers, with a small spoon for each colour. The paint should be the thickness of single cream.

3. Look at the salad spinner with the children and find out how it works.

4. Ask the children what they think would happen if you put paint in the salad spinner.

5. Put your first circle of paper in the spinner, drop some paint in from the spoons, and turn the handle.

6. Stop the spinner and see what has happened. The paint should have spun into a pattern. Take the paper out and look at it.

7. Now let the children experiment with the spinner and the different colours of paint. Add some glitter or confetti after the first spin.

8. Think of other things you could use in the salad spinner: cotton wool balls, leaves, a sponge ball, a 'koosh' ball or one with spikes on it. Use soft things, or slow down as you spin harder things like marbles.

Top tip ⭐

Don't forget to wash your spinner after you have finished or it will clog up with paint and won't work!

Taking it forward

- Put some water or thin paint in a bucket on the patio or playground. Dip the ends of long bits of string or rope in the bucket. Hold the dry end and spin round, drawing on the ground as you spin.

What's in it for the children?

Simple experiments help children to understand how materials behave.

It's windy!

Use plastic carriers to have some fun in the wind.

What you need:

- Carrier bags
- String or wool
- Scissors
- A superhero figure

Taking it forward

- Make more things for the superheroes: houses, tents, hammocks, cloaks, masks and vehicles.

- Make a PowerPoint presentation about superheroes, with photos of them flying, using their parachutes, or standing in their tents. Add a few words to each photo and share the presentation with the class.

What's in it for the children?

Using characters from popular culture draws children in to activities that they may not choose voluntarily.

✚ Health & Safety
Make sure children know not to put carrier bags over their heads.

What to do:

This activity has two outcomes – a kite, and a parachute for a superhero.

A kite

1. Tie a length of string to the handles of a carrier bag – thin bags work better!

2. Cut some strips from another bag, or a black bin liner, and tie these to the handles too.

3. Go out and try your kite by running along, pulling it behind you. In a good wind and with a long string it will fly well.

A parachute

1. Cut a square from the side of a thin carrier bag.

2. Cut four strings, all about 35 cm long.

3. Tie one string to each corner of the plastic square.

4. Tie two of the strings around the superhero's wrists, and two around his shoulders.

5. Go out and carefully climb up a climbing frame, a tree, or a stepladder.

6. Throw your superhero into the air and see him float down on his parachute!

Top tip ⭐
Ask parents to collect bags for you.

Plaster fun
Simple work with plaster

What you need:

- Plaster of Paris
- Water
- Bowls for mixing
- A selection of beads, sequins and other small decorative items
- Old pencils
- Food colouring or thin paint

What to do:

1. Talk about making some decorative plaques for your room or outdoor area. Look at the plaster, and explain that it is a very quick drying mixture that builders use to make walls flat and neat. It dries very quickly, so the children must be ready to start as soon as the plaster is mixed.

2. Make sure everything is ready, and the children have a plastic tray and access to the decorative items.

3. Now let them watch as you measure and mix the plaster. Depending on the number of children, you may need to make more than one batch. Wash the mixing bowl in a bucket of water between batches.

4. Pour the plaster into the plastic trays and let the children immediately start to add decorative things – they will have about five minutes!

5. Gently feel the plaster in the tray – it will get warm.

6. Watch and feel as the plaster hardens. You will be able to remove the plaques in about ten minutes, and put them somewhere safe to completely harden.

7. When the plaques are completely dry, the children can paint them – thin paint is easier, as it doesn't obscure the decorations.

8. Stick the plaque onto wood or thick card to display it.

Top tip ⭐

Never tip spare plaster down the sink - it will set and block the drains! Wait till it sets in the bowl and pop it out. Pour away waste plaster water outside (in small quantities it won't do any harm).

Taking it forward

- Make casts of toys or natural objects in small pots or cake cases to make badges, or to put on calendars or cards.

- Pour plaster in a tray and make marks with toy cars, or footprints of small world animals and people.

What's in it for the children?

Casting is a magical process and this is the first step in learning about it.

➕ **Health & Safety**

Remember not to pour plaster or plaster water down the sink.

Wet and wild
Throwing at a target

What you need:

- Several polystyrene pizza bases
- Thick permanent and water based markers
- Sponge balls
- A bucket
- Water
- Chalk
- A hammer and nails

Top tip ⭐

Ask families to collect the polystyrene backs from take-away pizzas, which are ideal for this activity.

Taking it forward

- Make some more targets with numbers on them. Use these for outdoor number practice.
- Make some more games for throwing: throw beanbags into buckets; put a basketball hoop up (not too high); get a children's football goal for your outdoor area to encourage goal scoring.

What's in it for the children?

Throwing games help co-ordination of hands and eyes, which in turn helps children with writing, reading and concentration.

✚ Health & Safety

Throwing games should always be sited towards a wall or fence to avoid accidents.

What to do:

1. Talk about what a target looks like, but be flexible if children have alternative ideas. Faces or other patterns can be just as much fun.

2. The children can make a target each or with a friend, then use them all for the game.

3. Paint doesn't stick very well on polystyrene, so use felt pens, or paint mixed with a lot of white glue or cornflour so it sticks better.

4. When the patterns are finished and dry, make a hole in the top of each target with an old pencil.

5. Help the children to hammer some nails into your fence or the side of a shed and hang your targets on the nails. Chalk a throwing line.

6. Fill a bucket with water and put three sponge balls in the water.

7. Take turns to throw three wet balls at the targets. How many can you hit?

8. Offer a clipboard and pens for scoring, or have a competition where the children work in pairs.

Sand tray town

Make a town in the sand tray

What you need:

- Your whole collection of building bricks
- A sand tray with some sand in it
- Scoops and sand tools

Top tip ⭐

While this activity is under way, offer sand for regular sand play in washing-up bowls or a builders' tray.

Taking it forward

- Sand and water trays can be used for other challenges, such as making an airport, a harbour, a space centre, a theme park, incorporating building bricks, small world toys and other resources in new ways.

- When the project loses its appeal, the demolition crew must do their work to wash the bricks and all the other equipment, maybe using a hose outside. The sand should be sieved into buckets or plastic boxes to remove leaves and stones. Then the crew can replace the sand ready for more play.

What's in it for the children?

Longer projects, lasting several days, can encourage creativity and deep involvement.

What to do:

1. This challenge should be started with a small group, but it will be very popular, so make sure that the children know there will be time for everyone to be involved as the building brick town develops.

2. Sit with the children near the sand tray and tell them you have another challenge for them. This time the challenge is to build a whole town in the sand tray.

3. Talk about what the town could look like, and what it needs. You could do a mind map of all the ideas, so you don't forget any of the suggestions.

4. Now let the work start. Stay near so you can contribute to the project, but don't take over.

5. One child could be asked to be the official photographer, and you could make a book about what happened.

6. Make sure that the children know they can incorporate other things in their project: natural objects such as sticks, twigs, leaves, gravel for paths, rocks and logs can be included and signs and notices can be made for your town.

7. The buildings will be made of building bricks, and there may be some boats, planes and other vehicles, but the children may want to use or make other things: people, cars, trees, black paper roads, silver foil for water, etc.

8. Give this project time to develop and make sure that everyone knows that it will change as other children join in.

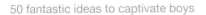

Pizza delivery
Make a take-away pizza

What you need:

- A trolley or set of drawers, table or desk, telephone
- A selection of pens and other mark makers, stapler, sticky notes, hole punch, ruler, calculator, clipboard
- Paper of all types and sizes
- Polystyrene circles from take-away or frozen pizzas
- Salt dough, paints
- Pizza boxes
- Bike or trike for deliveries

Top tip ⭐

Ask your local pizza seller to donate some pizza boxes.

Taking it forward

- If possible, make some real pizzas with ready-made pizza bases and real toppings.

What's in it for the children?

Real-life situations are ideal for role-play where children learn to talk and behave like adults.

 Health & Safety

Remove sim cards from phones. Make sure adults do the cooking.

What to do:

This activity is about replaying a familiar experience in role-play situation. It would be good to do during a project on 'Our community'.

1. Get permission from your manager to order a pizza for delivery to your setting. As you share the pizza, talk about how take-away services work.

2. Talk with the children about setting up a pizza delivery activity in your outdoor area, and take their suggestions seriously. Discuss where it should be and how it would work.

3. Let the children make some salt dough for pizzas, using:

   6 cups flour, 6 cups salt, 6 tablespoons vegetable oil, 3 cups warm water.

   Set up the pizza delivery in the agreed place, and let the children get involved in play.

4. Use the dough to make pizzas, and bake these in a slow oven until hard. Then paint them like pizzas and stick them on polystyrene pizza circles.

5. Let the children decide where the pizza place will be, how it will take orders and make deliveries, who will do the various jobs.

6. Add extras if children ask for them, and make a place to display notices, posters or any other writing they produce. Visit your pizza place and order a pizza yourself – talking to the children in role.

7. Talk about how the people in your home corner can order a pizza.

Catch a crawly
Jelly fishing game

What you need:

- A big container, such as a water tray, baby bath or paddling pool
- Lots of small world snakes, frogs, lizards, etc.
- Little fishing nets (from pet shops)
- Small bowls
- Gelatin
- Black food colouring, such as Edicol dye
- Water
- A two minute sand timer (optional)

What to do:

1. Fill the container with water. You could do this when the children have gone home, or do the whole thing with them.

2. Add food colouring to the water until is quite dark.

3. Mix the gelatin with warm water to dissolve it. Check the packet for amounts, and remember you only want the water to be slightly set, not stiff jelly!

4. Put the small world creatures in the jelly, and leave it for a few hours, or overnight, till slightly set.

5. Explain the game to the children, and they can get going independently. They each work with their own net to catch the creatures and put them in their own bowl. When the timer is finished, players count to see who has won. The winner gets to throw all the creatures back in the jelly!

6. A whiteboard and pen make a good score board.

Taking it forward

- Fishing games are good for fine motor skills and counting. Cut fish and sea creature shapes from heavy-duty carrier bags or polystyrene food trays and write numbers on them with a permanent marker. Float these in a water tray for fishing.

- Buy some little soy sauce fish or 'ball pool' balls from the Internet, number them and use these for a novel fishing game.

What's in it for the children?

Simple active games like this make learning about numbers much more fun.

Top tip ⭐

If you can't get black colouring, use other colours, adding them to the water until you get a dark mixture.

Battling cars

A car game that involves making and playing

What you need:

- Toy cars
- A large cardboard box
- Scissors
- Markers
- Some car magazines
- White glue or glue sticks
- Duct tape

What to do:

1. Talk with the children about making a game to play with cars. Collect some toy cars for the game.

2. Cut the flaps off a large box.

3. Draw several arches on one side of the box, along the open edge. Check that the cars would go through the arches and adjust the size if the arches are too small.

4. Help the children to cut out the arches.

5. Now find lots of pictures of cars and other vehicles in the magazines and cut or tear them out.

6. Stick the pictures all over the front of the box. If you have enough pictures, the children could cover the sides and top too. Draw and cut out a score number for each of the arches, and stick one above each arch.

7. When you have finished this stage, paint all over the pictures with dilute white glue. This will stick everything down and make the game stronger.

8. Draw a starting line for the cars and you are ready to play. This game is best played lying down!

Top tip ⭐

Ask parents for old car magazines.

Taking it forward

- Make more themed games for rolling or throwing. Use popular culture such as current superheroes, pop singers, TV celebrities or football players.

- Make some race games on big sheets of card, using cars or other small world figures such as zoo animals as playing pieces.

What's in it for the children?

This game is rooted in boys' interests – speed and competition.

Health & Safety

Remind the children never to aim the cars at each other, and watch out for small parts.

New from old

Use old crayon stumps in new activities

What you need:

- Use of an oven
- Old crayons, crayon stumps
- An old bun tin
- Zip-lock bags
- Big bricks or rolling pins

Taking it forward

- Make big crayons in foil dishes, with all the colours mixed. Try to fill the tins and use the new crayons outside.

- Grate crayons onto coffee filter papers and heat in a warm oven. When they cool, they will be like jewelled windows.

What's in it for the children?

This activity underlines the need to recycle materials and is a reminder that the outcomes can be surprising!

✚ Health & Safety

Children should stay away from hot surfaces.

What to do:

Talk with the children about recycling, and how you can make new things from old things.

1. Show the children how to peel the paper from the crayons making sure it is all removed.

2. Sort the crayons into colours and put each colour in a separate bag.

3. Close the bags and roll or bash them with bricks or rolling pins until the crayons are in tiny pieces.

4. Tip the colours into bun tins, keeping each colour separate. You may wish to line the tins first.

5. If you like, try a few mixtures – red and blue, yellow and blue, red and white – to make swirly new colours.

6. Put the bun tin in a warm oven (about 100°).

7. Watch carefully; the crayons will melt quite quickly.

8. Show the children the melted wax, but warn them not to touch it.

9. Leave the wax until it is cool, then pop the new round crayons out of the tins.

10. Use your new crayons for drawing different pictures. Talk about what has happened to the old crayons.

Rainmakers
Make a rainstick

Top tip ⭐
Use cardboard tubes from gift wrap to make really long rainsticks, or tape several tubes together.

What you need:

- **Rainstick** (as an example)
- **Cardboard tubes, 30–50 cm long** (e.g. from kitchen roll or foil)
- **Lots of small, short nails with heads, almost as long as the width of tubes you are using**
- **Hammers**
- **Thin card, masking or duct tape, glue sticks**
- **Rice or dried lentils**
- **A small jug**
- **Paint, foil, coloured sticky tape**

What to do:

1. Explain what a rainstick is, and show one if you can.

2. Help the children to hammer nails into the tube, until the heads are flush with the surface. They can hammer the nails anywhere they like, randomly or in patterns. More nails will make a better sound!

3. If the tube has no ends, show the children how to seal one end of the tube by drawing around the end onto a piece of card. Draw another circle outside the first one, and draw several wide spokes between the outer and inner circles. Cut around the outer circle, and then cut along all the spokes. Make another of these circles for the other end of the tube. Stand the tube on one circle, glue all the spokes and bend them up to stick onto the tube.

4. Fill the jug with rice or beans and pour them into the tube. You will have to experiment to find the right amount for the length of the tube: a small jug full should be about right.

5. Put your hand over the open end of the tube and try your rainstick by tipping it slowly upside down and listening. Does it have enough nails? Does it have enough rice or beans?

6. When you are happy with the sound, seal the end of the tube and decorate it with tape, paint, foil, stickers or anything else you like.

Taking it forward

- Make a didgeridoo from a long tube, decorate it and then find out how to play it.

- Make drums from plastic boxes or bowls by covering the top with cling film or a plastic bag, and securing this with tape or a strong elastic band.

What's in it for the children?

Making sounds with home-made instruments is a good way to get interested in music.

Health & Safety
Supervise children when using hammers.

Spiderworld!
Large-scale weaving outdoors

Top tip ⭐

Buy some plastic 'toilet step' stools for outdoor seats and steps.

What you need:

- Lots and lots of wool, string and ribbon:
  - unravel old knitted jumpers or scarves; ask families if they have any wool or string
  - look on market stalls and in charity shops; ask at wool shops and florists
  - buy big balls of garden string, raffia, gift string and embroidery silks
  - tear long fabric strips from big pieces of fabric, e.g. old sheets
  - try your local scrapstore or recycling centre
- Safe steps, stools and ladders
- Scissors

What to do:

1. Collect together the strings and wools and look at them with the children.

2. Suggest that the children could make their outdoor area into a 'spiderworld' by making webs everywhere. Ask them to suggest how they could go about making 'spiderworld'.

3. Work with them as they get busy, following their ideas and only intervening if things get difficult or risky.

4. Incorporate all the outside objects, climbing frames, fences and hedges, posts, roofs, sheds, bushes, drainpipes and gates.

5. Less adventurous children may want to work on a smaller scale, using thinner strings nearer to the ground and in secret corners.

6. Stand back with the children as the project develops, looking at the overall effect and thinking about whether it is finished yet.

7. Take plenty of photos; this project won't be sustainable for more than a few days.

8. When the webs are finished (or the strings have run out) let the children play Spiderman games in the new environment they have made.

9. When the 'spiderworld' has lost its appeal, or begins to look tired, wet or disappointing, prepare the children for dismantling it. The best way is to let them do it for themselves, with scissors and rubbish bags, restoring their play area to its original familiar form.

Taking it forward

- Make mini 'spiderworlds' in boxes, using sticks and branches, and thin wool or cotton. Dip thin string in glue and glitter to make the environments even more magical. Add small-world figures of Spiderman, or plastic spiders.

What's in it for the children?

This project shows children that they can transform their environment themselves.

Health & Safety

Risks are associated with using string and wool, but this is a wonderful project. Be vigilant.

Journey into space

Make a small world landscape

Top tip ⭐

Do this activity outside - it is messy!

What you need:

- A big sheet of plywood or thick card from the side of a large carton
- Lots of newspaper
- Masking tape
- Plaster bandage
- Aprons
- A bowl or bucket of water
- Scissors
- Small-world figures

Taking it forward

- Use your landscape as the inspiration for photo sequences, stories and other imaginative play.

- Make other landscapes as the children's interests or your topics change. This will ensure they are fully involved in cross-curricular activities.

What's in it for the children?

Small world play underpins storytelling and other creative thinking.

What to do:

1. Put on your aprons, and put the baseboard on the floor or a table out of doors.

2. Show the children the plaster bandage, and explain that it is often used to make plaster casts for people who have broken their arms or legs.

3. Talk with the children about using the plaster bandage to make a landscape for small-world figures, and ask them what sort of landscape they would like to make.

4. When you have agreed, begin to make the landscape by scrunching up newspaper to make hills and other features, sticking them down with masking tape.

5. Cut lengths of plaster bandage and work with the children to dip these in the water and drape them over the landscape you are making. Use your fingers to gently smooth the surface of the plaster, and to make rivers, beaches, valleys and roads. Wah your hands well afterwards!

6. When you are happy with the landscape, leave it to dry overnight, before adding trees, roads and other features with paint, gravel, sandpaper, foil, twigs and other natural materials.

Crazy dough

Use your food colours to mix a new sort of dough

What you need:

- 9 cups of plain white flour
- 4½ cups of salt
- 9 tablespoons of vegetable oil
- 9 tablespoons of cream of tartar
- 9 cups of warm water
- Food colouring (black, purple, brown) mixed with the water
- Mixing bowl, wooden spoon
- Cooking pan
- Dough tools: knives, sticks and other objects for shaping and moulding

Top tip ⭐

Buy used saucepans from charity shops or junk stalls for this activity.

Taking it forward

- There are many dough recipes that children can make independently. Make a book of recipes and ideas.
- Provide some more unusual tools such as a garlic press, textured rollers, themed cutters, pumpkin cutting tools in plastic and butter knives.

What's in it for the children?

This activity supports both independence and creativity.

⊕ Health & Safety

Keep children away from the heat source when you are mixing up the dough and baking the finished products.

What to do:

1. Let the children measure and mix the ingredients.

2. An adult can then heat the dough, stirring all the time, until it thickens and comes away from the edge of the pan. Remove the pan from the heat, tip the dough onto a table and leave to cool.

3. Break the dough into several pieces. The children will enjoy kneading it until it is smooth and shiny.

4. Now the children can experiment with the dough, making objects, creatures or ugly faces! They can work together on big pieces, but will need help to lift them onto a baking tray.

5. If they want to hang their creations up or wear them, they need to make one or more holes in the dough with a pencil.

6. Bake the creations in a low oven until they are hard. Reinforce that the children must watch this stage while the adults handle the hot materials.

7. Once cooled, the children can decorate their creations with paint, beads, sequins and other objects.

8. Create medals or necklaces by threading small dough objects on string or ribbon.

9. To make the creations extra hardwearing, paint them with thick PVA, which will go clear as it dries.